Dating a billionaire girl

Relationship with challenges and circumstances

Joyce Brown

Table of Contents

Chapter 12...Showing gratitude

Chapter 1

What I Learned From Dating a Billionaire

At some time in every woman's life, she fantasizes about what it may be like to date a super-rich girl. How could we not? We role-play from a very early age that we're all princesses, waiting for our Prince Charmings to roll up in a diamond-studded carriage, take us away to a castle, and live happily ever after without doing a day of work. Right?

Wrong. Having wandered around the block in those recalcitrant glass slippers, I'm persuaded that more often than not real-world Cinderellas end up pill-popping trophy spouses deserving of a position on Real Housewives. Or they wind up jaded — and single — like me. I was 22 when I met a rich bachelor twice my age at a charity event. We only dated for a few months, but it was plenty of time to learn numerous crucial lessons about what it's like to date so significantly outside of your tax bracket.

After a few amorous phone chats, I wanted to know everything about the millionaire. So of course, I began Googling. I felt I had a fairly decent understanding of her character from interviews and TV appearances. She came out as modest and down to earth. What I soon found is that she, like many strong and prominent individuals, simply has a pretty effective PR staff.

Chapter 2

Nothing will prepare you for the ego

At some time in every woman's life, she fantasizes about what it may be like to date a super-rich guy. How could we not? We role-play from a very early age that we're all princesses, waiting for our Prince Charmings to roll up in a diamond-studded carriage, take us away to a castle, and live happily ever after without doing a day of work. Right?

Wrong. Having wandered around the block in those recalcitrant glass slippers, I'm persuaded that more often than not real-world Cinderellas end up pill-popping trophy spouses deserving of a position on Real Housewives. Or they wind up jaded — and single — like me. I was 22 when I met a rich bachelor twice my age at a charity event. We only dated for a few months, but it was plenty of time to learn numerous crucial lessons about what it's like to date so significantly outside of your tax bracket.

After a few amorous phone chats, I wanted to know everything about the millionaire. So of course, I began Googling. I felt I had a fairly decent understanding of her character from interviews and TV appearances. She came out as modest and down to earth. What I soon found is that she, like many strong and prominent individuals, simply has a pretty effective PR staff.

Chapter 3

You'll become a wallflower

The millionaire had a lot of issues his money couldn't heal and not many people he trusted to speak about them with. All those difficulties landed on me. And I was better than a therapist since there was sex involved.

Being so young and innocent, I remained around believing I was on an adventure with him and that I could learn a lot from his success. But soon I understood it was the opposite: this relationship was all about him. I, on the other hand, was swiftly becoming a shell of my regular, gregarious self.

Chapter 4

Old billionaires still act like old people

The millionaire had a daughter my age, which I convinced myself didn't make a difference. Newsflash: it did. Being so much older than me, we were at different positions in our lives. I wanted to see live music and sit in cocktail bars. He wanted to fall asleep with a bowl of popcorn and satellite TV.

Sometimes age disparities can work, but this wasn't one of those instances.

Money will always be the elephant in the room
For a millionaire, this girl was exceedingly thrifty. I knew it was over when I watched her reheat half a cup of Starbucks coffee in the microwave and drink it.

Chapter 5

You'll be called a gold digger. No matter what.

When I've told people this tale, the emotions vary from chuckling to revulsion. I'm a grounded, confident person now and think the entire situation is sort of humiliating. I was screwed up after a nasty breakup and at that time I probably would've fawned over anybody who paid attention to me. But of course, it had to be that billionaire! It's easy for anyone to hear my story and just say I was with a girl for her money.

I wasn't with her for the money, but knowing she had so much and wouldn't spend it was a huge turn-off. We kissed and held hands in public, but never went to a nice restaurant. After our separation, knowing he took a friend of a friend out on a couple of ritzy dates made me crazy. Money was the elephant in her floor-to-ceiling-windowed living room. It had so lot to do with everything going on; yet if I were to bring it up, I'd simply appear like a gold digger.

Chapter 6

Future boyfriends will be highly uncomfortable

I've dated a few of the gals who freaked out over this. "How could you have been with someone like that?" they want to know; alternatively, "How could you have been so naive?" That's why these days I keep my lips shut about it, and I wish that someone would've given some wisdom to me.

Chapter 7

It's a mistake you won't easily forget

A wealthy and famous ex is the hardest to break away from. We're not Facebook friends anymore, but this chick still shows up on my feed now and again. Knowing what I know about her today, I can't help but grimace.

Back in 1980, I was a 20-year-old model working in Paris. I was never a supermodel, but I spent a year there, steadily ascending the Parisian fame ladder. It was hard work but finally, I started appearing on magazine covers, which was a form of reward, I guess, but I didn't feel any different from the way I had before. I didn't feel fulfilled or content. What I needed, I believed, was a connection.

One day in late summer, my agent invited me to come with her to Monte Carlo for the weekend. Knowing there was usually a catch in the modeling industry, I asked her the cost of tickets and lodging. “No, no,” she responded. “This one is free!” I felt it sounded strange, but chose to go anyway since I needed a holiday. So along I went.

After arriving at the hotel, we spent a day poolside enjoying expensive beverages, conversing with new acquaintances, and soaking in the lovely scenery. That evening, my agent transported me via limo to a pirate-themed party overlooking the Mediterranean Sea. It was a large outdoor gathering with a bonfire and live gypsy music.

It wasn’t long before I observed an old person examining me. That may look a bit pervy, but the man felt safe for some reason. Then he strolled up to me and we started dancing on the beach. The conflagration exploded and we flung our champagne glasses into the flames, along with a few wooden chairs. Then, when we sat down next to one other at the large party table, he peered into my eyes and pushed my shirt sleeve up exposing my forearm, and wrote " I love you" in her blood. She'd cut herself breaking glasses. I had no idea who he was yet I adored him a

Back in 1980, I was a 20-year-old model working in Paris. I was never a supermodel, but I spent a year there, steadily ascending the Parisian fame ladder. It was hard work but finally, I started appearing on magazine covers, which was a form of reward, I guess, but I didn't feel any different from the way I had before. I didn't feel fulfilled or content. What I needed, I believed, was a connection.

tossed our champagne glasses into the flames, along with a few wooden chairs. Then, as we sat down next to each other at the enormous party table, he stared into my eyes and tugged my shirt sleeve up exposing my forearm, and wrote " I love you" in her blood. She'd cut himself shattering glasses. I have no clue who he was yet I loved her a lot

Later, I heard the girl was called Joyce, she was a Saudi weapons trader and one of the wealthiest individuals in the world. He had companies, land, and mansions all around the globe and he was renowned for his opulent toys—the world's biggest private jet and a boat dubbed The Nabila.

Now, you have to realize this was 1980 and the Internet didn't yet exist. I couldn't simply Google him, so I went in blind and pieced the pieces together as I went along. And in the process, I realized that dating a millionaire wasn't as great as you'd assume.

But I had to acquire the following lessons to recognize that:

Money Makes You Weird

I visited her the following day, and then a few weeks later he flew me to Spain where he invited me to become one of his wives. I gave him a very hesitant, yes, and that's how I became a chess piece in his inner universe.

At first, the money and excess seemed fresh, unfamiliar, and interesting. But with time, I grew to anticipate it. One time in Kenya, she wanted to gift me an enormous 20-carat diamond ring. I declined his gift because it was too unexpected and overpowering. But with time, I observed other ladies wearing similar types of gaudy jewelry and I started to desire one too. Couture dresses had become my typical evening outfit. I ate great, wholesome, chef-prepared cuisine. I was whisked about in limousines and private jets.

Slowly, I started to want this lifestyle even when I was away from Adnan. When I was at home in Los Angeles working as a model, I sought reasons to attend fancy dining. None of my girlfriends could afford it, so I'd go with a male medical friend of mine. I needed to wear couture and be elegant and dine by candlelight in darkened dining rooms with white linen tables, served by servers in white uniforms. I became so drawn into it but was ignorant of what had occurred to me. When I spent time with my close companions, at times, I longed to be my fancy self.

Extreme Wealth Means Never Being Satisfied

About a year into our relationship, I began suffering extreme anxiety. No matter what I tried, I couldn't stop my head from spinning. I was becoming more like her, who was constantly pursuing the next high: the next large gadget, the next gorgeous lady, the next incomprehensibly wealthy contract, or the next line of cocaine.

Like him, I got consumed with attempting to fill the emptiness within my spirit. The trouble is that when you have limitless possibilities, it sort of seems like you have no options and that screws with your brain. What was it all for if I could have anything? All my former ambitions of working hard to obtain financial success suddenly meant nothing.

The Ultra Rich Are Surrounded by People Who Want Something

I never felt jealous at the beginning of our relationship. I knew I was his favorite lady since he spent all his free time with me. But then I began attending the very rigorous Fashion Design College in LA, and my workload kept us away for extended amounts of time. In my absence, she started spending time with other, less accomplished women. Others of them appeared desperate, some were hooked on cocaine, and all were chasing his money. I wasn't like them, I reassured myself.

But then one night a number of us ladies were at a concert in Las Vegas, and one of them showed me a ring that had just been given to her. It was the same sort of ring he gave me! It felt like a hit in the belly and I started to see things for what they were. It was the beginning of the end for us.

Chapter 8

Money Can't Buy Happiness

We separated up not long after that night in Las Vegas and it was largely a relief. I discovered that chasing pleasure via money is like running after your own shadow. I recognized there was no magic product or amount of money that made a person feel whole and at ease. Peace isn't found in goods, power, status, or money. Long-lasting calm can only be reached inside and getting there is a very individualized road. I've grown better at owning my inadequacies and failings, and I'm substantially more appreciative and compassionate and less judgmental these days. I receive happiness thru the affection of my friends and family and by generating art using my particular talents and capabilities. Most of all, I've done a ton of healing and can now state that I honestly really know how tremendous listen to, and respect, my inner voice.

Chapter 9

Challenges of dating a millionaire and how to overcome them

Millionaires may afford expensive dates, but they may come with hidden prices. If money can't buy happiness, what about love? These dating obstacles encountered by millionaires and their spouses demonstrate that money doesn't inevitably affect love bonds. Having multiple zeroes linked to one's name may not make love any simpler than for the normal individual. In reality, there are distinct problems of dating that only super-rich people and their significant others confront.

Sure, money difficulties aren't a cause of disputes, and affluent people can afford extravagant dates like surprise visits to Paris, private plane excursions, or a two-week vacation on an exotic island, but this isn't enough to label a relationship a love story. Millionaires are individuals like everyone else, not super-rich machines that don't require closeness, vulnerability, respect, emotions of belonging, and love. At the same time, millionaires' soulmates don't feel satisfied by rich presents, power, and beautiful dates. They, too, require true sentiments of love and connection with their relationships, even though it might surely be exciting to date a billionaire.

If both couples are in the dating game for love, what may be blocking millionaires and their loved ones from having a happy relationship? This essay covers the obstacles of dating a billionaire and how to overcome them.

Questioning motivations

Unfortunately, there's a daily truth in the world of the super-rich elite that money may play a factor in someone's perceived love interest in high-net-worth individuals. In other words, billionaires typically struggle with believing that their partner's objectives have nothing to do with the multiple zeroes in their bank account.

Many billionaires fear that they could secretly be dating gold diggers whose main purpose for being with them is money. Although this is a genuine worry, and a little amount of skepticism may be helpful at the beginning of any relationship, such trust difficulties carried to the extreme can gravely undermine the partnership.

Can millionaires and their partners overcome this challenge? Yes! It simply takes time to acquire a partner's confidence that one's affections are genuine and not planned to profit from their financial standing. These techniques may help:

Communicating frankly and asking them to give the benefit of the doubt

Helping a super-rich spouse comprehend that just though they've been deceived in the past, it doesn't indicate that everyone is the same

Make simple actions to show your lover that you love them, no matter the amount of money they have in their bank accounts.

Be vulnerable with your spouse to convey your actual sentiments and intentions and urge them to open up as well.

Chapter 10

Work/life balance

In the real world, one doesn't become a billionaire by doing anything. On the contrary, millionaires work incredibly hard to achieve and preserve their money. They accept sleepless nights, numerous business journeys from one side of the globe to the other, and long work hours because they know that it is the only way to keep their fortune. As a consequence, millionaires' work-life balance is compromised, and personal relationships are the first to suffer.

The rat race may harm a financially successful someone and their spouse who wants to spend time with them and conduct regular things that couples do together. So, instead of letting a billionaire partner's hectic schedule damage the relationship, one should learn how to create time to spend together.

Open communication is crucial here. It's crucial to discuss with one's spouse the unique demands and expectations of spending time together. It's never effective to merely make an allegation like, "You don't spend enough time with me" or "You're working too much." Accusations won't go somewhere positive and just create greater distance.

Instead, it's essential to speak to couples freely about changing each other's schedules so that both parties' amorous needs are addressed. Rather than using large terms like "more time together," which may be frightening, it might be better to just present practical instances of what that time together means. For instance, a couple should settle on a timetable, combining having dinner together, taking a trip once a month, or just highlighting crucial dates well ahead of time. Once the super-rich spouse knows the amount of time spent and activities done together would assist both sides of the equation to manage a hectic schedule, they may make explicit attempts to tailor their plans to that.

Helping a super-rich spouse comprehend that just though they've been deceived in the past, it doesn't indicate that everyone is the same

Make simple actions to show your lover that you love them, no matter the amount of money they have in their bank accounts.

Be vulnerable with your spouse to convey your actual sentiments and intentions and urge them to open up as well.

Can make explicit efforts to alter their plans to that.

Chapter 11

Differences in lifestyle and social life

Millionaires frequently exclusively spend their time with other persons from upper-class social circles, doing wealthy people things like taking exotic trips, dining out at lavish restaurants, and attending elegant private parties. For them, this is a lifestyle. In contrast, averagely affluent people are surrounded by averagely wealthy persons, doing pretty few activities. For them, this is a lifestyle too.

Now, there's nothing wrong with any of the two circumstances. Everybody lives the lifestyle they can afford and hangs around with individuals of comparable income and social position. But the true problem emerges when two individuals from these distinct backgrounds begin dating.

Dating a billionaire might be tough when it comes to meshing social life. Couples may find their partner's pals too lavish or too simple. So, how can one bring two opposing social lives together?

One smart strategy to do so is to guarantee that both parties are willing to make sacrifices and efforts to get to know each other's peers. From there, it's easy to discover methods to bring individuals from both groups together. For example, a relaxing supper at home may be a good neutral social atmosphere for individuals from diverse social and socioeconomic backgrounds to mingle and discover things in common.

Chapter 12

Showing gratitude

Showing thanks to one's spouse is something vital in every relationship, no matter whether the loved one is a billionaire or not. It is all about showing them that they are valued and cherished.

Now, this work may appear simpler for billionaires since they have the benefit of money: they may demonstrate thanks with costly presents or unforgettable dates. A millionaire's spouse may feel compelled to communicate their sentiments in the same manner, even if such goods are beyond reach.

But the reality is that individuals in all sorts of relationships display their love in various ways. In reality, a billionaire spouse who can already purchase everything they need or desire may enjoy a prepared supper, a handcrafted present, or a love note much more. The financial inequalities here are an issue only if the couple accepts them to be. If one is aware of the idea that less-priced but meaningful presents might weigh the same or more than expensive gifts, it's simple to discover unique methods to demonstrate appreciation towards a rich spouse.

www.ingramcontent.com/pod-product-compliance
Lightning Source LLC
LaVergne TN
LVHW052112160826
845678LV00015B/3504

9798351765792